Serving the Lord with a Willing Heart

A 12-Week Bible Study on Faithful Service for the Lord

DR. LENDE CLICK

Copyright Page

Dedication

This Bible study is dedicated first and foremost to my Lord and Savior, Jesus Christ.

Lord, every word, every lesson, and every page belongs to You. Thank You for calling Your daughters to serve You with willing hearts, humble hands, and faithful love.

I also dedicate this book to every woman who serves the Lord in quiet and hidden places.

To the woman who prays when no one sees,
to the woman who helps without needing applause,
to the woman who keeps serving even when she feels tired,
to the woman who gives, encourages, teaches, cleans, cooks, comforts, and loves in the name of Jesus—

God sees you.
God remembers your labor of love.
Your service is not small when it is done for Him.

May this Bible study remind you that every act of obedience, every humble assignment, and every willing yes to God matters in the Kingdom of Heaven.

"And whatsoever ye do, do it heartily, as to the Lord, and not unto men."
— Colossians 3:23 KJV

Introduction

Serving the Lord is one of the greatest honors of a believer's life.

Many people think serving God means having a title, standing on a platform, leading a large ministry, or being seen by others. But the heart of true service is much deeper than that.

Serving the Lord begins with a willing heart.

A woman can serve Jesus while teaching His Word, but she can also serve Him while praying quietly, encouraging someone who is hurting, preparing a meal, cleaning a room, helping at church, caring for her family, visiting the lonely, or doing a small task with love.

When it is done for Jesus, it matters.

God does not measure service the way people often do. People may notice the big things, but God sees the hidden things. He sees the prayer whispered in secret. He sees the tired hands that keep serving. He sees the kind words spoken to a wounded heart. He sees the quiet obedience no one else applauds.

Nothing done for the Lord is wasted.

This 12-week Bible study was written to encourage women to serve Jesus with humility, joy, faithfulness, and love. Each week will guide you through Scripture, reflection, prayer, personal application, and simple weekly challenges to help you grow in faithful service.

You do not need to be famous to be faithful.
You do not need a platform to be used by God.
You do not need applause to please the Lord.

All you need is a heart that says, "Lord, use me."

As you walk through this study, may the Lord remind you
that your service matters. Whether your assignment feels big
or small, visible or hidden, easy or difficult, God sees your
heart.

May this Bible study strengthen your faith, refresh your spirit,
and encourage you to keep serving the Lord with a willing
heart.

*"And whatsoever ye do, do it heartily, as to the Lord,
and not unto men."*
— Colossians 3:23 KJV

How to Use This Bible Study

This Bible study was created to help you grow in faithful service to the Lord Jesus Christ.

Each week is designed to guide you through Scripture, reflection, prayer, personal application, and a simple challenge that helps you live out what you are learning.

You may complete one lesson each week by yourself, with a friend, or in a women's Bible study group.

There is no need to rush. Take your time with each lesson. Read the Scriptures slowly. Pray before you begin. Ask the Holy Spirit to speak to your heart and show you how to serve the Lord with greater humility, joy, love, and faithfulness.

Each week includes:

Main Scripture
A Bible verse that gives the main focus for the week.

Memory Verse
A short Scripture to remember and carry in your heart.

Opening Prayer
A prayer to help you begin the lesson with a surrendered heart.

Opening Thought
A short encouragement to prepare your heart for the weekly teaching.

Lesson

A teaching section that explains the weekly theme and how it applies to serving the Lord.

Key Truth

A simple truth to remember throughout the week.

Bible Reading

Additional Scriptures to read, study, and pray over.

Reflection

A deeper heart-focused section to help you examine your walk with God.

Bible Study Questions

Questions to help you think, write, and personally apply God's Word.

Heart Check

A time to prayerfully examine your motives, attitudes, and willingness to serve.

Personal Application

A practical way to apply the lesson to your life.

Weekly Challenge

A simple step of obedience to help you serve the Lord in everyday life.

Prayer

A closing prayer is connected to the weekly lesson.

Declaration of Faith
A faith-filled statement to speak over your life.

Notes
Space to write thoughts, prayers, Scriptures, or anything the
Lord places on your heart.

As you go through this Bible study, remember this: serving the
Lord is not about being perfect. It is about being willing.

God can use a willing heart.
God can use small acts of obedience.
God can use hidden service.
God can use ordinary moments for His glory.

Before each lesson, pray this simple prayer:

*Lord Jesus, open my heart to Your Word. Teach me to
serve You with humility, joy, and love. Use my life
for Your glory. In Jesus' name, Amen.*

Table of Contents

Week 1:

Called to Serve the Lord

Main Scripture

"I beseech you therefore, brethren, by the mercies of God, that ye present your bodies a living sacrifice, holy, acceptable unto God, which is your reasonable service."
— Romans 12:1 KJV

Memory Verse

"Present your bodies a living sacrifice, holy, acceptable unto God."
— Romans 12:1 KJV

Opening Prayer

Lord Jesus,

Thank You for calling me to serve You. Help me to understand that my life belongs to You. Teach me to give You my heart, my hands, my time, my gifts, and my obedience.

Remove anything in me that serves only for attention, approval, or recognition. Give me a willing heart that says yes to You.

Lord, use my life for Your glory. Teach me to serve with humility, joy, love, and faithfulness.

In Jesus' name,
Amen.

Opening Thought

Before we can truly serve the Lord with our hands, we must first surrender our hearts.

Serving God is not only about what we do in church. It is not only about standing in front of people, teaching, singing, preaching, leading, or being noticed. Serving the Lord begins when we offer our whole life to Him.

Romans 12:1 reminds us to present our bodies as a living sacrifice. That means our daily life becomes an offering to God. Our words, our attitude, our work, our kindness, our forgiveness, our obedience, and even our small responsibilities can become worship when they are given to the Lord.

God is not only looking for talented people. He is looking for surrendered people.

A willing heart is precious to God.

Lesson: Service Begins with Surrender

Many people want to serve God, but true service begins with surrender.

To surrender means to say, "Lord, my life belongs to You. Use me the way You want to use me."

When we surrender to God, we stop asking only, "What do I want to do?" and we begin asking, "Lord, what do You want me to do?"

Sometimes God may call us to serve in visible ways. Other times, He may call us to serve in quiet and hidden ways. Both matter to Him.

A woman who teaches a Bible study is serving the Lord.
A woman who cleans the church is serving the Lord.
A woman who prays for others is serving the Lord.
A woman who encourages the brokenhearted is serving the Lord.
A woman who prepares food for someone in need is serving the Lord.
A woman who cares for her family with love is serving the Lord.
A woman who forgives when it is hard is serving the Lord.

When it is done for Jesus, it is not small.

People may judge service by position, title, or visibility. But God looks at the heart.

Key Truth

You are not called to serve for applause. You are called to serve the Lord.

When your service flows from a surrendered heart, even ordinary work becomes holy.

Bible Reading

Read the following Scriptures slowly and prayerfully:

Romans 12:1–2
Colossians 3:23–24
Matthew 20:26–28
1 Samuel 16:7
Psalm 100:2

Reflection: What Is God Asking Me to Surrender?

Serving the Lord requires a heart that is willing to be shaped by Him.

Sometimes we must surrender pride.
Sometimes we must surrender fear.
Sometimes we must surrender the need to be noticed.
Sometimes we must surrender comparison.
Sometimes we must surrender our own plans.

A surrendered heart says:

"Lord, I am available."
"Lord, I am willing."
"Lord, teach me."
"Lord, correct me."
"Lord, use me."
"Lord, let my life bring You glory."

God can do beautiful things through a woman who is willing to obey Him.

Bible Study Questions

1. According to Romans 12:1, what are we called to present to God?

____

____

____

2. What does it mean to you to be a "living sacrifice" for the Lord?

____

____

____

3. Why do you think service must begin with surrender?

____

____

4. Read Colossians 3:23–24. How should this Scripture change the way we do everyday work?

____

____

5. What is one small assignment in your life that you sometimes overlook, but God may see as important?

____

____

6. Have you ever felt that your service was not noticed by people? How does it encourage you to know that God sees?

____

____

7. What attitude do you need God to help you change as you serve Him?

____

____

8. What area of your life do you need to surrender more fully to the Lord?

____

____

____

Heart Check

Take a moment and prayerfully ask yourself:

Am I serving the Lord with joy?
Am I serving because I love Jesus?
Am I serving to be seen by people?
Am I comparing my assignment to someone else's?
Am I willing to serve even when no one notices?
Am I giving God my whole heart or only part of it?

Personal Application

This week, ask the Lord to show you one way you can serve Him with a willing heart.

It may be something simple:

Encourage someone.
Pray for someone.
Help someone quietly.
Serve in your home with joy.
Complete a small responsibility without complaining.

Thank someone who serves faithfully.
Do a hidden act of kindness.

Write one specific way you will serve the Lord this week:

Weekly Challenge

This week, do one act of service for the Lord without telling anyone.

Let it be between you and Jesus.

After you do it, write how it affected your heart:

Prayer

Lord Jesus,

I give You my heart again today. I surrender my life, my time, my gifts, my hands, and my service to You.

Teach me to serve with humility. Teach me to serve with joy. Teach me to serve even when no one sees. Help me remember that my work is not wasted when it is done for You.

Remove pride from my heart. Remove comparison from my heart. Remove the desire to be praised by people. Give me a pure and willing heart.

Lord, use me in small ways and big ways. Use my life to bless others and glorify Your name.

I am Yours.
My service belongs to You.

In Jesus' name,
Amen.

Declaration of Faith

I am called to serve the Lord.
My life belongs to Jesus.
My work has purpose when it is done for Him.
I do not need applause to be faithful.
God sees my heart.
God sees my service.
Even small things matter when they are done for the Lord.

Notes

Week 2:
Faithful in Small Things

Main Scripture

"He that is faithful in that which is least is faithful also in much."
— Luke 16:10 KJV

Memory Verse

"He that is faithful in that which is least is faithful also in much."
— Luke 16:10 KJV

Opening Prayer

Lord Jesus,

Thank You for reminding me that small things matter to You. Help me not to despise small assignments, quiet service, or hidden work.

Teach me to be faithful where You have placed me. Give me a humble heart that serves You with joy, even when the task feels simple or unnoticed.

Lord, help me remember that when I serve with love, I am serving You.

In Jesus' name,
Amen.

Opening Thought

Sometimes people think the big assignments matter more than the small ones. But in the Kingdom of God, faithfulness matters more than size.

God sees the small acts of obedience. He sees the quiet prayers. He sees the helping hands. He sees the woman who keeps showing up, keeps loving, keeps serving, and keeps doing what is right even when no one applauds her.

A small job done with a faithful heart is a big thing before God.

Lesson: God Honors Faithfulness

Jesus said that the person who is faithful in little will also be faithful in much. This teaches us that God does not only look at the size of the assignment. He looks at the heart of the servant.

Before God gives someone more, He often watches how they handle what is already in their hands.

Can they serve without complaining?
Can they be trusted with small responsibilities?

Can they honor God when no one is watching?
Can they stay faithful when the work feels hidden?

Faithfulness is not always loud. Sometimes faithfulness looks like doing the same simple thing with love, patience, and obedience.

A woman who prepares a meal with love is serving.
A woman who cleans a room for God's house is serving.
A woman who calls to encourage someone is serving.
A woman who prays for her family is serving.
A woman who teaches one child about Jesus is serving.
A woman who welcomes people with kindness is serving.
A woman who gives her time quietly is serving.

These things may look small to people, but they are not small to God.

The Lord can take small obedience and turn it into great blessing.

Key Truth

Small assignments become sacred when they are done faithfully for the Lord.

God is not asking us to be famous. He is asking us to be faithful.

Bible Reading

Read the following Scriptures slowly and prayerfully:

Luke 16:10

Matthew 25:21

Zechariah 4:10

Colossians 3:23–24

Galatians 6:9

Reflection: Do Not Despise Small Beginnings

The Bible says, **"For who hath despised the day of small things?"** *– Zechariah 4:10 KJV*

Sometimes we look at our assignment and think, "This is not much." But God may be using that small beginning to prepare something greater in us.

Small beginnings can build strong character.
Small assignments can teach humility.
Small acts of service can strengthen faith.
Small steps of obedience can open bigger doors.

God often begins with the small because He is building the heart first.

Before David became king, he served in the field with sheep. Before he stood before a nation, he was faithful in a hidden place. God saw him there.

In the same way, God sees you.

He sees your prayers.
He sees your tears.
He sees your obedience.
He sees your serving.
He sees your love.
He sees your faithfulness.

Nothing done for Jesus is wasted.

Bible Study Questions

1. According to Luke 16:10, what does faithfulness in small things reveal about a person?

2. Why do you think God cares about how we handle small assignments?

3. What is one small responsibility in your life that
God may be using to grow your character?

____

____

____

4. Read Matthew 25:21. What did the master say to the
faithful servant?

____

____

____

5. Have you ever felt like your service was too small to
matter? Explain.

____

____

____

6. How does Zechariah 4:10 encourage you about
small beginnings?

____

____

____

7. What is one area where you need to become more
faithful, even when no one notices?

____

____

____

8. How can you serve this week with a better attitude and a more willing heart?

____

____

____

Heart Check

Take a moment and prayerfully ask yourself:

Am I faithful in small things?
Do I complain when the task feels little?
Do I compare my assignment to someone else's?
Do I serve only when people notice?
Do I believe God sees my hidden work?
Am I willing to honor God in ordinary responsibilities?

Personal Application

This week, choose one small assignment and do it with excellence for the Lord.

It may be:

Cleaning something with joy.
Helping someone without being asked.
Praying for someone faithfully.
Serving in church with humility.
Encouraging one person.

Finishing a task you have been avoiding.
Showing kindness to someone who cannot repay you.

Write your small assignment for this week:

____

____

____

Weekly Challenge

This week, take one ordinary task and turn it into worship.

Before you do it, pray:

"Lord, I do this for You."

Afterward, write what God showed you:

____

____

____

Prayer

Lord Jesus,

Help me to be faithful in small things. Forgive me for the times
I have overlooked small assignments or thought they did not
matter.

Teach me to serve You with joy in ordinary places. Help me to remember that nothing done for You is wasted. Give me patience when my work feels hidden. Give me humility when my assignment feels small. Give me strength to keep serving with love.

Lord, I want to be faithful where You have placed me. Use my small obedience for Your glory.

In Jesus' name,
Amen.

Declaration of Faith

I will be faithful in small things.
I will not despise small beginnings.
My service matters to God.
My hidden work is seen by Heaven.
I do not need a big platform to obey the Lord.
Small obedience can carry great purpose.
I will serve Jesus with a willing heart.

Notes

Week 3:

Working for the Lord, Not for People

Main Scripture

"And whatsoever ye do, do it heartily, as to the Lord, and not unto men."
— Colossians 3:23 KJV

Memory Verse

"Whatsoever ye do, do it heartily, as to the Lord, and not unto men."
— Colossians 3:23 KJV

Opening Prayer

Lord Jesus,

Thank You for reminding me that my work and service belong to You. Help me not to serve only for approval, praise, or recognition from people.

Teach me to do everything with a sincere heart, knowing that You see me. Help me serve with excellence, love, and humility, even when no one thanks me or notices my effort.

Lord, let my work become worship before You.

In Jesus' name,
Amen.

Opening Thought

It is easy to become discouraged when people do not notice what we do. Sometimes we serve, give, help, clean, pray, encourage, teach, or sacrifice, and no one says thank you.

But Colossians 3:23 reminds us that our work is not only for people. It is for the Lord.

When we remember that Jesus is the One we are serving, our attitude changes. We no longer depend on human applause to keep going. We serve because we love Him.

People may overlook your labor, but God never does.

Lesson: Serving with the Right Focus

When we work for the Lord, our service becomes worship.

There is a difference between serving to be seen and serving because we are surrendered. A person can do the right work with the wrong heart. That is why God cares not only about what we do, but why we do it.

If we serve only for people's approval, we may become hurt
when they do not appreciate us. If we serve only to be noticed,
we may become discouraged when someone else receives
attention. If we serve only for praise, we may stop when the
praise stops.

But when we serve the Lord, our strength comes from Him.

A willing servant says:

"Lord, I am doing this for You."
"Lord, I want my heart to please You."
"Lord, even if no one sees, You see."
"Lord, let this work bring You glory."

This does not mean people should never encourage or
appreciate one another. Encouragement is beautiful. But our
service should not depend on human praise.

Jesus is worthy of our best, even in small things.

When you clean, clean for the Lord.
When you teach, teach for the Lord.
When you cook, cook for the Lord.
When you help, help for the Lord.
When you pray, pray for the Lord.
When you lead, lead for the Lord.
When you serve your family, serve for the Lord.
When you serve in ministry, serve for the Lord.

When your heart is focused on Jesus, ordinary work becomes
holy.

Key Truth

When I serve for the Lord, my work becomes worship.

People may not always see my labor, but God sees my heart.

Bible Reading

Read the following Scriptures slowly and prayerfully:

Colossians 3:23–24

Ephesians 6:7

Galatians 1:10

Matthew 6:1

Hebrews 6:10

Reflection: Who Am I Trying to Please?

One of the greatest heart checks in service is this question:

Am I doing this for God, or am I doing this to be seen by people?

This question may feel uncomfortable, but it is important. The Lord wants to purify our motives. He wants our service to come from love, not pride. He wants our obedience to come from worship, not performance.

Sometimes we may begin serving with a pure heart, but over time we can become tired, hurt, or hungry for recognition. We may wonder, "Does anyone even see what I do?"

God sees.

He sees the prayers no one heard.
He sees the tears no one noticed.
He sees the work no one thanked you for.
He sees the kindness no one repaid.
He sees the sacrifice no one understood.

When you serve for the Lord, nothing is wasted.

Bible Study Questions

1. According to Colossians 3:23, how should we do our work?

2. What does it mean to work "as to the Lord, and not unto men"?

3. Have you ever felt discouraged because your service was not appreciated? What happened?

4. Read Ephesians 6:7. What kind of attitude should we have when serving?

5. Why is it dangerous to serve only for human approval?

6. Read Matthew 6:1. What warning does Jesus give about doing good works to be seen by people?

7. What is one area where you need to shift your focus back to the Lord?

8. How can you remind yourself this week that your service is for Jesus first?

____

____

____

Heart Check

Take a moment and prayerfully ask yourself:

Am I serving the Lord or trying to impress people?
Do I become upset when no one notices my work?
Do I compare my service to someone else's?
Am I giving Jesus my best, even in small things?
Do I need people's praise to keep serving?
Is my work becoming worship before the Lord?

Personal Application

This week, before you begin a task, pause and say:

"Lord Jesus, I do this for You."

Say it before you clean, cook, help, teach, pray, write, serve, encourage, or work.

Write one task you will intentionally do for the Lord this week:

____

____

Weekly Challenge

Choose one responsibility this week that you normally do without much joy. Instead of rushing through it or complaining, do it as worship to the Lord.

Ask God to change your attitude while you do it.

Afterward, write what changed in your heart:

____

____

____

Prayer

Lord Jesus,

Forgive me for the times I have served with the wrong focus. Forgive me for wanting praise more than wanting to please You.

Clean my heart. Purify my motives. Teach me to serve You with sincerity, humility, and love.

Help me remember that You see what others do not see. You know the labor, the sacrifice, the prayers, the tears, and the obedience.

Let my work become worship. Let my service bring You glory. Whether people notice or not, I want to be faithful to You.

In Jesus' name,
Amen.

Declaration of Faith

I work for the Lord, not for people.
My service belongs to Jesus.
My work can become worship.
I do not need applause to obey God.
The Lord sees my heart.
The Lord sees my labor.
I will serve faithfully, with joy and humility.

Notes

Week 4:

Serving with a Pure Heart

Main Scripture

"Take heed that ye do not your alms before men, to be seen of them: otherwise ye have no reward of your Father which is in heaven."
— Matthew 6:1 KJV

Memory Verse

"Take heed that ye do not your alms before men, to be seen of them."
— Matthew 6:1 KJV

Opening Prayer

Lord Jesus,

Thank You for teaching me that service is not about being seen by people, but about pleasing You.

Search my heart and remove anything that is not pure before You. Take away pride, selfish motives, comparison, and the desire for attention. Teach me to serve with humility, love, and sincerity.

Let my service be a sweet offering to You.

In Jesus' name,
Amen.

Opening Thought

God is not only looking at what we do. He is looking at why
we do it.

A person can do a good thing with the wrong motive.
Someone can give, help, pray, serve, or work in ministry, but
still desire attention, praise, or recognition more than the glory
of God.

Jesus taught us to be careful not to do righteous acts just to be
seen by people. This does not mean our service must always
be hidden. It means our heart must be pure.

The question is not only, "What am I doing?"
The deeper question is, "Who am I doing this for?"

Lesson: God Sees the Motive

People see the outside, but God sees the heart.

Sometimes people can see our hands serving, but only God
can see the reason behind the service. He knows when we
serve out of love. He knows when we serve out of pride. He
knows when we serve with joy. He knows when we are only
trying to be noticed.

A pure heart says:

"Lord, I want You to be glorified."
"Lord, I want to serve because I love You."
"Lord, I do not need attention."
"Lord, clean my motives."
"Lord, let people see You, not me."

Serving with a pure heart does not mean we are perfect. It means we are willing to let God correct us, humble us, and cleanse us.

There may be times when our motives need to be checked. We may ask ourselves:

Am I serving because I love Jesus?
Am I serving because I want people to admire me?
Am I hurt because I was not praised?
Am I comparing my service to someone else's?
Am I trying to prove something?

These questions are not meant to condemn us. They are meant to help us grow.

A willing servant lets the Lord purify the heart.

Key Truth

Pure service is not about being seen by people; it is about being pleasing to God.

When the heart is clean before the Lord, the service becomes beautiful.

Bible Reading

Read the following Scriptures slowly and prayerfully:

Matthew 6:1–4
1 Samuel 16:7
Psalm 139:23–24
Proverbs 16:2
Colossians 3:23

Reflection: Let God Search the Heart

David prayed, "Search me, O God, and know my heart." — Psalm 139:23 KJV

That is a brave prayer. It invites God to examine what is inside us. It asks Him to reveal anything that does not please Him.

Sometimes we do not even fully understand our own motives. We may think our heart is completely pure, but God may gently show us places where pride, hurt, fear, or insecurity has entered.

The Lord does not reveal these things to shame us. He reveals them to heal us and make us more like Jesus.

When God purifies our hearts, our service becomes lighter. We no longer serve under pressure to impress people. We no longer need to compete. We no longer need to be praised. We can simply serve because we love the Lord.

A pure heart brings peace to service.

Bible Study Questions

1. According to Matthew 6:1, what does Jesus warn us not to do?

2. Why do you think God cares about the motive behind our service?

3. Read 1 Samuel 16:7. What does this verse teach us about how God sees people?

4. Have you ever served and secretly wanted people to notice or thank you? What did God teach you?

5. What is the difference between serving to glorify God and serving to impress people?

6. Read Psalm 139:23–24. Why is it important to ask God to search our hearts?

7. What motive do you need to surrender to the Lord this week?

8. How can you serve with a purer heart in your home, church, ministry, or community?

Heart Check

Take a moment and prayerfully ask yourself:

Am I serving with a pure heart?
Do I want God to be glorified more than I want to be noticed?
Do I get upset when people do not thank me?
Am I serving from love or from pride?

Am I comparing my service with someone else's?
Do I need God to clean my motives?

Personal Application

This week, pray before you serve and ask the Lord to purify your heart.

Pray this simple prayer:

"Lord, let my service be for You and not for attention."

Write one area where you want God to purify your motive:

____

____

____

Weekly Challenge

This week, do one act of service quietly without trying to be noticed.

It may be:

Praying for someone secretly.
Helping someone without announcing it.
Giving quietly.
Cleaning or preparing something without seeking praise.
Encouraging someone without expecting anything back.

Afterward, write what God showed you about your heart:

Prayer

Lord Jesus,

Search my heart and make it clean before You. Forgive me for the times I have served with pride, comparison, or a desire to be noticed.

Teach me to serve because I love You. Help me to do good without needing applause. Help me to give without needing recognition. Help me to obey without needing praise.

Make my service pure. Make my heart humble. Make my motives pleasing to You.

Let my life point people to You, not to me.

In Jesus' name,
Amen.

Declaration of Faith

I will serve with a pure heart.
I will not serve for attention.
I will not serve for applause.
I will serve because I love Jesus.
God sees my heart.

God knows my motives.
My service is an offering to the Lord.

Notes

____

____

____

____

____

____

____

____

____

____

Week 5:
Using What God Has Given You

Main Scripture

"As every man hath received the gift, even so minister the same one to another, as good stewards of the manifold grace of God."
— 1 Peter 4:10 KJV

Memory Verse

"As every man hath received the gift, even so minister the same one to another."
— 1 Peter 4:10 KJV

Opening Prayer

Lord Jesus,

Thank You for the gifts, talents, abilities, and experiences You have placed in my life. Help me not to hide what You have given me. Teach me to use every gift with humility, love, and faithfulness.

Show me how to serve others with what is already in my hands. Let my gifts bring glory to You and encouragement to Your people.

In Jesus' name,
Amen.

Opening Thought

God did not give you gifts by accident.

Every ability, every talent, every experience, every lesson, and every testimony can be used for His glory. Sometimes we look at what others can do and forget to value what God has placed inside of us.

But the Lord does not ask us to use someone else's gift. He asks us to be faithful with what He has given us.

Your gift may be teaching.
Your gift may be encouraging.
Your gift may be praying.
Your gift may be serving quietly.
Your gift may be hospitality.
Your gift may be giving.
Your gift may be listening.
Your gift may be helping.
Your gift may be writing.
Your gift may be comforting the hurting.

Whatever God has placed in your hands, He can use it for His Kingdom.

Lesson: Your Gift Is for God's Glory

First Peter 4:10 teaches that every person has received a gift and should use it to minister to others. This means our gifts are not only for ourselves. They are given so we can bless, serve, strengthen, and encourage others.

A gift becomes ministry when it is offered to God.

Sometimes people hide their gifts because they feel afraid. They may think:

"I am not good enough."
"Someone else can do it better."
"What if people judge me?"
"What if I make a mistake?"
"My gift is too small."

But God is not asking for perfection. He is asking for willingness.

When Moses felt unqualified, God still called him.
When David was overlooked, God still chose him.
When Esther was afraid, God still positioned her.
When the boy had only five loaves and two fish, Jesus still used what he had.

God can multiply what is surrendered.

Do not bury your gift because of fear. Do not compare your gift to another woman's gift. Do not despise what God has placed in you.

Your gift has purpose. Your testimony has purpose. Your service has purpose.

When you use what God has given you with a humble heart, you become a vessel of His grace.

Key Truth

God gave me gifts so I can serve others and glorify Him.

My gift may look small to people, but in God's hands, it can become a blessing.

Bible Reading

Read the following Scriptures slowly and prayerfully:

1 Peter 4:10–11

Romans 12:6–8

1 Corinthians 12:4–7

Matthew 25:14–30

2 Timothy 1:6–7

Reflection: What Is in Your Hands?

When God called Moses, He asked him, **"What is that in thine hand?"** *— Exodus 4:2 KJV*

Moses had a rod. It looked simple, ordinary, and unimpressive. But when surrendered to God, that rod became part of a mighty deliverance.

Sometimes we are waiting for something bigger, while God is asking us to use what we already have.

What is in your hands?

A voice that can encourage.
Hands that can help.
A heart that can pray.
A home that can welcome.
A story that can give hope.
Wisdom that can guide.
A skill that can serve.
A testimony that can strengthen someone else.

The enemy wants women to hide their gifts because of fear, shame, insecurity, or comparison. But the Lord calls His daughters to rise up and be faithful stewards of what He has entrusted to them.

Your gift does not have to look like someone else's gift to be valuable.

God gave it to you for a reason.

Bible Study Questions

1. According to 1 Peter 4:10, what should we do with the gift we have received?

____

____

____

2. What gift, ability, or experience has God placed in your life that can bless others?

____

____

____

3. Have you ever compared your gift to someone else's gift? How did that affect you?

____

____

____

4. Read Romans 12:6–8. What different kinds of gifts are mentioned in these verses?

____

____

____

5. Why do you think fear causes many people to hide their gifts?

____

____

____

6. Read 2 Timothy 1:6–7. What does Paul encourage Timothy to do with the gift of God?

7. What is one gift you need to "stir up" again and use for the Lord?

8. How can you use what God has given you this week to serve someone else?

Heart Check

Take a moment and prayerfully ask yourself:

Am I using what God has given me?
Am I hiding my gift because of fear?
Am I comparing my gift to someone else's?
Do I believe my gift matters to God?
Am I willing to serve others with humility?
Have I thanked God for what He placed in my hands?

Personal Application

This week, ask the Lord to show you one gift, ability, or experience He wants you to use for His glory.

Write it here:

____

____

____

Now write one practical way you can use it this week:

____

____

____

Weekly Challenge

This week, use one gift God has given you to bless someone else.

You may:

Pray for someone.
Encourage someone with kind words.
Cook or prepare something for someone.
Teach or share a Scripture.
Help someone with a need.
Write a note or message of encouragement.
Serve quietly in your church, home, or community.

Afterward, write what happened and how it made you feel:

Prayer

Lord Jesus,

Thank You for the gifts You have placed in my life. Forgive me for the times I have hidden them because of fear, insecurity, comparison, or doubt.

Help me to be a faithful steward of what You have given me. Teach me to use my gifts with humility and love. Let my gifts bless others, strengthen Your people, and bring glory to Your name.

Lord, stir up what You have placed inside of me. Give me courage to serve. Give me wisdom to use my gifts well. Give me a willing heart that says yes to You.

Everything I have came from You, and I give it back to You for Your glory.

In Jesus' name,
Amen.

Declaration of Faith

God has given me gifts for His glory.
I will not hide what He placed in me.
I will not compare my gift to someone else's.

I will use what is in my hands.
My gift can bless others.
My testimony can encourage others.
My service matters to God.
I will be a faithful steward of His grace.

Notes

Week 6:
God Sees the Hidden Servant

Main Scripture

"For God is not unrighteous to forget your work and labour
of love, which ye have shewed toward his name."
— Hebrews 6:10 KJV

Memory Verse

"God is not unrighteous to forget your work and labour of
love."
— Hebrews 6:10 KJV

Opening Prayer

Lord Jesus,

Thank You for seeing what others may never see. Thank You
for remembering every act of love, every prayer, every
sacrifice, and every service done for Your name.

Encourage my heart when I feel unnoticed. Strengthen me
when I feel weary. Teach me to serve faithfully, even in hidden
places, knowing that nothing done for You is ever forgotten.

In Jesus' name,
Amen.

Opening Thought

There are many servants of God who serve in quiet places.

They may not stand on a platform.
They may not receive applause.
They may not be publicly thanked.
They may not be seen by many people.

But they are seen by God.

Hebrews 6:10 reminds us that God does not forget our work and labor of love. People may forget. People may overlook. People may not understand the cost. But the Lord remembers.

Hidden service is not wasted service.

When it is done for Jesus, Heaven sees it.

Lesson: Heaven Keeps Record

Sometimes the most faithful servants are the ones working behind the scenes.

They prepare the room before others arrive.
They pray when no one knows.
They clean when everyone leaves.
They encourage the hurting quietly.
They give without announcing it.
They serve their families faithfully.
They show kindness when no one is watching.
They keep obeying God when no one claps.

The world often celebrates what is visible, but God honors what is faithful.

A hidden servant may feel forgotten, but she is not forgotten by the Lord. God sees the love behind the labor. He sees the tired hands. He sees the faithful heart. He sees the sacrifice. He sees the tears.

And He remembers.

Jesus Himself spent many years in hidden preparation before His public ministry began. He knew what it meant to live faithfully in ordinary places. He knew what it meant to serve without seeking attention.

If Jesus valued humble service, then we should value it too.

Sometimes God hides His servants not because they are unimportant, but because He is forming something deep within them.

The hidden place can produce humility.
The hidden place can build character.
The hidden place can strengthen faith.
The hidden place can purify motives.
The hidden place can prepare a servant for greater obedience.

Never believe the lie that hidden means useless.

Hidden roots hold up strong trees.

Key Truth

God sees every hidden act of faithful service, and He does not forget.

Even when people overlook your labor, Heaven remembers your love.

Bible Reading

Read the following Scriptures slowly and prayerfully:

Hebrews 6:10
Matthew 6:4
Colossians 3:23–24
Psalm 139:1–3
Galatians 6:9

Reflection: Seen by God

There is a holy comfort in knowing that God sees.

He sees when you keep serving after disappointment.
He sees when you love people who do not thank you.
He sees when you pray through tears.
He sees when you give from a place of sacrifice.
He sees when you choose humility instead of pride.
He sees when you keep showing up.

The enemy may whisper, "No one cares. No one sees. This does not matter."

But God's Word says something different.

God sees.
God remembers.
God rewards.
God is pleased by faithful love.

You may feel hidden from people, but you are never hidden from God.

Bible Study Questions

1. According to Hebrews 6:10, what does God not forget?

2. What does "labor of love" mean to you?

3. Have you ever served in a way that felt unnoticed? How did it affect your heart?

4. Read Matthew 6:4. What does Jesus teach about
what is done in secret?

5. Why do you think hidden service can sometimes be
difficult?

6. How does it encourage you to know that God
remembers your work?

7. What hidden place of service has God called you to
be faithful in right now?

8. How can you continue serving with joy, even when
people do not notice?

Heart Check

Take a moment and prayerfully ask yourself:

Do I feel discouraged when people do not notice my service?
Am I still willing to serve in hidden places?
Do I believe God remembers my labor of love?
Have I allowed bitterness to enter because I felt overlooked?
Am I serving for Heaven's approval or people's attention?
Can I trust God with what no one else sees?

Personal Application

This week, write down one hidden act of service you have done or are currently doing for the Lord.

Now write a prayer of surrender, giving that service back to God:

Weekly Challenge

This week, encourage one person who serves quietly.

It may be someone who cleans, helps, prays, prepares, gives, teaches, welcomes, cooks, organizes, or serves behind the scenes.

Tell her:

"I see your faithfulness, and I believe God sees it too."

Afterward, write what happened:

____

____

____

Prayer

Lord Jesus,

Thank You for seeing me in hidden places. Thank You for remembering what others may forget.

Forgive me for the times I became discouraged because I wanted people to notice. Heal my heart from any hurt, bitterness, or weariness that came from feeling overlooked.

Teach me to serve with joy, even when my work is quiet. Help me remember that Heaven sees what people miss. Strengthen my hands and renew my heart.

Lord, let my hidden service be a beautiful offering to You.

In Jesus' name,
Amen.

Declaration of Faith

God sees my hidden service.
God remembers my labor of love.
I am not forgotten.
My quiet obedience matters.
My hidden work has purpose.
I will not serve for applause.
I will serve faithfully for the Lord.
Heaven sees what people may overlook.

Notes

Week 7:
The Ministry of Helping

Main Scripture

"And God hath set some in the church, first apostles,
secondarily prophets, thirdly teachers, after that miracles,
then gifts of healings, helps…"
— 1 Corinthians 12:28 KJV

Memory Verse

"God hath set some in the church… helps."
— 1 Corinthians 12:28 KJV

Opening Prayer

Lord Jesus,

Thank You for reminding me that helping others is holy work.
Teach me not to look down on simple acts of service. Help me
to see that every time I help with love, I am serving You.

Give me willing hands, a humble heart, and eyes that notice
the needs around me. Use me to strengthen, encourage, and
bless others for Your glory.

In Jesus' name,
Amen.

Opening Thought

Helping may seem small to some people, but in the Kingdom of God, helping is a ministry.

Not everyone is called to stand in front of a crowd, but every believer can help. A helping hand can lift a burden. A kind word can strengthen a weary soul. A simple act of service can show the love of Jesus.

The Bible includes **helps** among the gifts God placed in the church. That means helping is not unimportant. It is part of God's design for His people.

When you help with love, you are doing Kingdom work.

Lesson: Helping Is Holy Work

Many people want visible assignments, but the ministry of helping often happens quietly. Helpers may not always receive recognition, but their work is deeply needed.

Helpers make ministry stronger.
Helpers lighten heavy loads.
Helpers bring comfort to the weary.
Helpers notice what others miss.
Helpers serve where there is a need.
Helpers reflect the servant heart of Jesus.

Jesus Himself helped people everywhere He went. He helped the sick. He helped the hungry. He helped the broken. He helped the rejected. He helped those who had no one to defend them.

Helping is not beneath a servant of God. Helping is one of the ways we become more like Christ.

Sometimes helping looks like:

Preparing a meal.
Cleaning a room.
Watching a child.
Praying for a friend.
Giving someone a ride.
Visiting the lonely.
Encouraging the discouraged.
Helping at church.
Listening with compassion.
Serving behind the scenes.

These things may look ordinary, but when they are done in love, they become sacred.

The ministry of helping reminds us that service is not always about having a title. Sometimes the greatest ministry is simply seeing a need and responding with love.

Key Truth

Helping others with love is a ministry that honors God.

When I help someone, I can become a vessel of God's kindness.

Bible Reading

Read the following Scriptures slowly and prayerfully:

1 Corinthians 12:27–28
Galatians 5:13
Philippians 2:3–4
Hebrews 13:16
Matthew 25:35–40

Reflection: Seeing the Need

A helper has eyes that notice.

Sometimes people around us are carrying burdens we cannot
see. They may be tired, lonely, grieving, overwhelmed,
discouraged, or silently praying for help.

A willing servant asks:

"Lord, who needs encouragement today?"
"Lord, who needs prayer today?"
"Lord, who needs help today?"
"Lord, how can I show Your love today?"

Helping does not always require money, position, or special
training. Sometimes it only requires a willing heart and
available hands.

A small act of help can become an answer to someone's
prayer.

God can use your kindness to remind someone that they are not alone.

Bible Study Questions

1. According to 1 Corinthians 12:28, what gift or ministry is included in the church?

2. Why do you think helping others is important in the Body of Christ?

3. Have you ever been blessed because someone helped you? What did it mean to you?

4. Read Galatians 5:13. How are we called to serve one another?

5. What are some simple ways women can help in the home, church, ministry, or community?

____

____

____

6. Read Philippians 2:3–4. What does this Scripture teach about considering the needs of others?

____

____

____

7. What need has God been placing on your heart to notice or help with?

____

____

____

8. How can helping others make us more like Jesus?

____

____

____

Heart Check

Take a moment and prayerfully ask yourself:

Do I notice the needs around me?
Am I willing to help even when it is inconvenient?

Do I look down on simple acts of service?
Do I wait for a title before I serve?
Am I helping with love or with complaint?
Can God trust me to respond when He shows me a need?

Personal Application

This week, ask the Lord to show you one person you can help.

Write the person's name or situation here:

____

____

____

Write one practical way you can help:

____

____

____

Weekly Challenge

This week, do one helpful act without waiting to be asked.

You may:

Help someone carry a burden.
Send an encouraging message.
Pray with someone.
Prepare something for someone.

Offer your time.
Help at church.
Visit or call someone who feels alone.
Clean or organize something that blesses others.

Afterward, write what God showed you:

____

____

____

Prayer

Lord Jesus,

Thank You for showing me that helping is holy work. Forgive
me for the times I overlooked the needs around me or thought
small acts of service did not matter.

Give me a heart that notices. Give me hands that are willing.
Give me compassion for those who are tired, hurting, lonely,
or overwhelmed.

Use me to help others in Your name. Let my service reflect
Your love. Let my kindness encourage someone's heart.

Teach me to serve without pride, without complaint, and
without needing recognition.

In Jesus' name,
Amen.

Declaration of Faith

Helping is a ministry.
My hands can serve the Lord.
My kindness can bless others.
God can use me to lighten someone's burden.
I will not wait for a title to serve.
I will notice the needs around me.
I will help with love and humility.
I will serve Jesus by serving others.

Notes

Week 8:
Serving Like Jesus

Main Scripture

"If I then, your Lord and Master, have washed your feet; ye
also ought to wash one another's feet."
— John 13:14 KJV

Memory Verse

"Ye also ought to wash one another's feet."
— John 13:14 KJV

Opening Prayer

Lord Jesus,

Thank You for being the perfect example of humble service.
You are Lord, King, and Master, yet You humbled Yourself
and served others with love.

Teach me to serve like You. Remove pride from my heart. Give
me humility, compassion, patience, and love. Help me not to
think any act of service is beneath me when it brings glory to
You.

In Jesus' name,
Amen.

Opening Thought

Jesus did not only teach about service. He showed us how to serve.

In John 13, Jesus washed His disciples' feet. This was a humble task, yet the Son of God did it with love. He was not trying to prove Himself. He already knew who He was. Because He was secure in the Father, He could serve with humility.

True service does not come from weakness. It comes from a heart surrendered to God.

Jesus showed us that greatness in the Kingdom is not measured by how many people serve us, but by how willing we are to serve others.

Lesson: The Servant Heart of Jesus

When Jesus washed the disciples' feet, He gave them a living example of humility.

He was their Lord and Master, yet He knelt before them. He held the towel. He washed dusty feet. He served the very men who would soon struggle, fail, and scatter.

This is the heart of Christ.

Jesus did not serve only those who were easy to love. He served imperfect people. He served people who did not fully understand Him. He served people who would disappoint Him.

Serving like Jesus means we must be willing to serve with humility, even when it is not glamorous. It means we do not need to be above others. It means we can love, help, forgive, and serve without needing to be praised.

A servant heart says:

"Lord, make me humble."
"Lord, teach me to love like You."
"Lord, help me serve without pride."
"Lord, let me see people through Your eyes."
"Lord, use my hands to bless others."

Jesus never treated humble service as shameful. He made it holy.

When we serve like Jesus, we reflect His heart to the world.

Key Truth

To serve like Jesus, I must be willing to love with humility.

True greatness in God's Kingdom is found in serving others.

Bible Reading

Read the following Scriptures slowly and prayerfully:

John 13:1–17
Matthew 20:26–28

Philippians 2:5–8
Mark 10:45
Luke 22:26–27

Reflection: No Assignment Is Beneath a Humble Heart

Pride says, "That job is beneath me."
Humility says, "Lord, if it honors You, I am willing."

Sometimes the Lord may ask us to serve in ways that challenge our pride. He may ask us to help someone quietly, forgive someone, clean up after others, encourage someone who never encouraged us, or serve without recognition.

These moments reveal the condition of our hearts.

Jesus did not come to be served, but to serve. If the King of kings humbled Himself, then we can humble ourselves too.

Serving like Jesus does not mean allowing people to abuse or mistreat us. It means we serve from love, wisdom, and obedience to God — not pride, bitterness, or the need for attention.

A humble servant knows her worth in Christ. She does not serve because she is less valuable. She serves because she belongs to Jesus.

Bible Study Questions

1. According to John 13:14, what did Jesus say His disciples ought to do?

2. Why was it powerful that Jesus, the Lord and Master, washed His disciples' feet?

3. What does Jesus' example teach us about humility?

4. Read Matthew 20:26–28. What does Jesus teach about greatness?

5. Have you ever struggled with feeling that a certain task was beneath you? What did God show you?

6. Read Philippians 2:5–8. How did Jesus humble Himself?

7. What is one way you can serve with more humility this week?

8. How can serving like Jesus change your home, church, ministry, or community?

Heart Check

Take a moment and prayerfully ask yourself:

Do I serve with the humility of Jesus?
Do I ever think certain tasks are beneath me?
Am I willing to serve when no one praises me?
Do I serve imperfect people with love?
Am I secure enough in Christ to humble myself?
Does my service reflect the heart of Jesus?

Personal Application

This week, ask the Lord to show you one way to serve with humility.

It may be:

Doing a task no one wants to do.
Helping someone who cannot repay you.
Encouraging someone who feels forgotten.
Serving without announcing it.
Forgiving someone who disappointed you.
Choosing kindness instead of pride.

Write one humble act of service you will do this week:

Weekly Challenge

This week, practice "towel service."

A towel represents humble service, just like Jesus washing the disciples' feet. Choose one simple, humble task and do it joyfully for the Lord.

Afterward, write what God taught you:

Prayer

Lord Jesus,

Thank You for showing me what true service looks like. You humbled Yourself, loved deeply, and served faithfully.

Forgive me for the times pride has entered my heart. Forgive me for thinking certain tasks were beneath me. Teach me to serve with a heart like Yours.

Help me to love imperfect people. Help me to serve without needing attention. Help me to stay humble, gentle, patient, and willing.

Let my life reflect Your servant heart.

In Jesus' name,
Amen.

Declaration of Faith

I will serve like Jesus.
I will walk in humility.
No act of service is beneath me when it honors God.
I am secure in Christ.
I can serve without needing applause.
I can love imperfect people with the love of Jesus.
True greatness is found in serving others.
My hands are available for the Lord's work.

Notes

Week 9:
Serving When You Feel Tired

Main Scripture

"And let us not be weary in well doing: for in due season we shall reap, if we faint not."
— Galatians 6:9 KJV

Memory Verse

"Let us not be weary in well doing."
— Galatians 6:9 KJV

Opening Prayer

Lord Jesus,

Thank You for understanding my weakness and weariness. You know when my heart feels tired, when my body needs rest, and when my spirit needs encouragement.

Strengthen me today. Teach me to serve from Your strength and not only from my own. Help me not to give up in doing good, but also teach me to rest wisely in Your presence.

Refresh my heart and renew my joy.

In Jesus' name,
Amen.

Opening Thought

Even faithful servants can become tired.

Loving people can be tiring. Serving in ministry can be tiring.
Carrying responsibilities at home, church, work, and family
can feel heavy. Sometimes a woman may keep pouring out to
others while quietly wondering, "Lord, who will pour back
into me?"

God is not harsh with tired servants. He is compassionate.

Galatians 6:9 encourages us not to become weary in doing
good. But this does not mean we should ignore rest or pretend
we are never tired. It means we must learn to keep our hearts
anchored in the Lord, trusting Him to strengthen us as we
continue to obey.

God does not only call us to serve. He also invites us to come
to Him and be refreshed.

Lesson: God Strengthens the Weary Servant

There is a difference between being tired and giving up.

A servant may feel tired and still love the Lord. A woman may
feel weary and still be faithful. A tired season does not mean
you are failing. It may simply mean you need to come closer to
Jesus and receive His strength.

Sometimes we become weary because:

We are doing too much without rest.
We are serving from pressure instead of love.
We are carrying burdens God did not ask us to carry.
We are trying to please everyone.
We are serving while wounded.
We are giving out but not being filled by the Lord.

Jesus understands weariness. He often withdrew to pray. He made time to be with the Father. He taught His disciples to come apart and rest.

Rest is not laziness when it is done in obedience to God. Rest can be wisdom. Rest can be healing. Rest can be preparation for continued service.

A willing servant must learn to say:

"Lord, strengthen me."
"Lord, refresh me."
"Lord, show me what is mine to carry."
"Lord, help me serve with joy, not resentment."
"Lord, teach me to rest without guilt."

Serving the Lord should not destroy the servant. God cares about the work, but He also cares about the worker.

When you are tired, do not run away from God. Run to Him.

Key Truth

God does not abandon His tired servants; He strengthens, refreshes, and renews them.

You can serve faithfully, but you must also rest wisely.

Bible Reading

Read the following Scriptures slowly and prayerfully:

Galatians 6:9
Isaiah 40:29–31
Matthew 11:28–30
Mark 6:31
Psalm 23:1–3

Reflection: Come to Jesus and Be Renewed

*Jesus said, **"Come unto me, all ye that labour and are heavy laden, and I will give you rest."** — Matthew 11:28 KJV*

That invitation is for the tired servant too.

Sometimes we think we must be strong all the time. We may feel guilty for needing rest. We may think that if we pause, we are disappointing God. But Jesus never asked us to serve without depending on Him.

He is the source of our strength.

When we serve from our own strength, we become drained quickly. But when we serve from our relationship with Jesus, He renews us.

The Lord knows how to restore the soul. He knows how to bring peace back to a weary heart. He knows how to give fresh joy to tired hands.

Do not be ashamed to tell the Lord, "I am tired."

He already knows, and He cares.

Bible Study Questions

1. According to Galatians 6:9, what are we encouraged not to do?

2. What does this verse promise will happen "in due season" if we do not faint?

3. Have you ever felt weary while doing good? What made you feel that way?

4. Read Isaiah 40:29–31. What does God give to the faint and weary?

5. Why is it important for servants of God to rest and be refreshed?

6. Read Matthew 11:28–30. What does Jesus invite the weary to do?

7. What is one burden you may be carrying that the Lord is asking you to give to Him?

8. What is one practical way you can receive rest and renewal this week?

Heart Check

Take a moment and prayerfully ask yourself:

Am I serving from God's strength or only from my own?
Am I tired because I am doing too much?
Am I carrying something God did not ask me to carry?
Do I feel guilty when I rest?
Have I allowed weariness to turn into resentment?
Am I coming to Jesus for renewal?

Personal Application

This week, write down one area where you feel tired or weary.

____

____

____

Now write one way you will bring that weariness to Jesus:

____

____

____

Weekly Challenge

This week, choose one intentional time of rest with the Lord.

You may:

Read a Psalm slowly.
Sit quietly in prayer.
Take a peaceful walk and talk to Jesus.
Listen to worship music.
Write in your journal.
Turn off distractions for a short time.
Ask God to restore your joy.

Afterward, write what God spoke to your heart:

____

____

____

Prayer

Lord Jesus,

I come to You tired, but trusting. You know every burden I carry. You know the places where I feel weary, stretched, and empty.

Forgive me for trying to serve in my own strength. Forgive me for carrying what You never asked me to carry. Teach me to serve faithfully, but also to rest wisely.

Restore my soul. Renew my joy. Strengthen my hands. Refresh my heart. Help me not to grow weary in doing good.

Lord, I receive Your rest, Your peace, and Your strength.

In Jesus' name,
Amen.

Declaration of Faith

God gives strength to the weary.
I do not have to serve in my own strength.
Jesus invites me to rest in Him.
My labor for the Lord is not wasted.
I will not give up in doing good.
I will rest without guilt.
I will serve from a renewed heart.
The Lord restores my soul.

Notes

Week 10:

Serving in Your Home, Church, and Community

Main Scripture

"But as for me and my house, we will serve the LORD."
— Joshua 24:15 KJV

Memory Verse

"As for me and my house, we will serve the LORD."
— Joshua 24:15 KJV

Opening Prayer

Lord Jesus,

Thank You for the places You have planted me. Thank You for my home, my family, my church, my work, and my community.

Open my eyes to see where You want me to serve. Teach me that ministry can happen in everyday places. Help me not to overlook the people closest to me.

Let my life bring honor to You wherever I go.

In Jesus' name,
Amen.

Opening Thought

Sometimes we think ministry only happens at church, on a platform, or in an official position. But serving the Lord can happen anywhere a willing heart obeys God.

You can serve Jesus in your home.
You can serve Jesus in your church.
You can serve Jesus in your workplace.
You can serve Jesus in your neighborhood.
You can serve Jesus in your community.

A kind word, a meal prepared with love, a prayer whispered for someone, a visit to the lonely, a helping hand, a clean room, a patient response, or a faithful responsibility can all become service to the Lord.

Wherever God has placed you, there is purpose.

Lesson: Your Place Is Your Mission Field

Joshua declared, **"As for me and my house, we will serve the LORD."** This was not only a statement of belief. It was a decision for his household to honor God.

Service often begins at home.

It is easy to want to serve people far away while overlooking the people closest to us. But God cares about how we love and serve in our own homes too. The way we speak, help, forgive, encourage, pray, and show patience can become part of our faithful service.

Your home can be a place of ministry.
Your kitchen can become a place of service.
Your table can become a place of encouragement.
Your prayers can cover your family.
Your kindness can change the atmosphere.

The church is also a place where believers serve together. Not everyone has the same assignment, but every part matters. Some teach. Some pray. Some welcome. Some clean. Some give. Some organize. Some visit. Some encourage. Some serve quietly behind the scenes.

And beyond the home and church, God may use you in your community. There are hurting people, lonely people, discouraged people, and people who need to see the love of Jesus through your life.

You do not need a title to serve.
You need a willing heart.

Key Truth

Where God has placed me, I can serve Him faithfully.

My home, church, and community can become places where God's love is shown through me.

Bible Reading

Read the following Scriptures slowly and prayerfully:

Joshua 24:15
Matthew 5:16
Galatians 5:13
Romans 12:10–13
Titus 2:3–5

Reflection: Ministry in Everyday Places

Ministry is not always loud. Sometimes it looks very ordinary.

It may look like folding laundry with prayer.
It may look like preparing food for someone who is tired.
It may look like helping at church without complaining.
It may look like speaking kindly when you feel frustrated.
It may look like visiting someone who feels forgotten.
It may look like praying for your pastor, family, friends, or neighbors.
It may look like encouraging another woman to keep trusting God.

The Lord can turn ordinary places into holy places when our hearts are surrendered to Him.

A faithful servant does not wait for a perfect place. She serves God where she is.

Ask the Lord:

"Who is near me that needs love?"
"What assignment is already in front of me?"
"How can I bring Your light into this place?"
"How can my home honor You?"
"How can I serve my church with humility?"
"How can I bless my community?"

God may use your everyday obedience more than you realize.

Bible Study Questions

1. According to Joshua 24:15, what decision did Joshua make for his household?

2. Why do you think serving the Lord should begin in the home?

3. What are some simple ways you can serve your family or household with love?

4. Read Matthew 5:16. How can our good works point people to God?

5. What is one way you can serve faithfully in your church?

6. Read Romans 12:10–13. What kinds of service and love are described in these verses?

7. Who in your community may need encouragement, prayer, or help?

8. What is one place where God has planted you that you need to see as a mission field?

Heart Check

Take a moment and prayerfully ask yourself:

Do I serve faithfully in my home?
Do I overlook the people closest to me?
Do I serve in church with humility and joy?
Do I notice needs in my community?
Am I waiting for a bigger platform while ignoring the assignment in front of me?
Does my everyday life point people to Jesus?

Personal Application

This week, write down one way you can serve in each area:

My home:

____

____

My church:

____

____

My community:

____

____

Weekly Challenge

This week, choose one act of service in your home, church, or community and do it with joy for the Lord.

You may:

Pray over your home.
Prepare a meal for someone.
Help with a church need.
Encourage a neighbor.
Call someone who feels alone.
Offer help without being asked.
Speak life over your family.
Serve quietly behind the scenes.

Afterward, write what God showed you:

____

____

____

Prayer

Lord Jesus,

Thank You for placing me where I am. Help me not to miss the ministry right in front of me.

Teach me to serve You in my home, in my church, and in my community. Let my words bring peace. Let my hands bring help. Let my prayers bring covering. Let my kindness show Your love.

Forgive me for overlooking small assignments or the people closest to me. Give me a faithful heart where You have planted me.

Use my everyday life for Your glory.

In Jesus' name,
Amen.

Declaration of Faith

I can serve the Lord where I am.
My home can honor God.
My church service matters.
My community can be touched by God's love.
I do not need a platform to be faithful.
I will serve with joy, humility, and love.
Where God has planted me, I will shine for Him.
As for me and my house, we will serve the Lord.

Notes

Week 11:
Your Labor Is Not in Vain

Main Scripture

"Therefore, my beloved brethren, be ye stedfast, unmoveable, always abounding in the work of the Lord, forasmuch as ye know that your labour is not in vain in the Lord."
— 1 Corinthians 15:58 KJV

Memory Verse

"Your labour is not in vain in the Lord."
— 1 Corinthians 15:58 KJV

Opening Prayer

Lord Jesus,

Thank You for reminding me that my labor for You is never wasted. Even when I do not see the fruit right away, help me to trust that You are working.

Strengthen my heart to remain steadfast and faithful. Teach me to keep serving, keep loving, keep praying, and keep obeying, knowing that everything done for You has purpose.

In Jesus' name,
Amen.

Opening Thought

Sometimes we serve, pray, give, help, teach, encourage, and sacrifice, but we do not always see immediate results.

We may wonder if our work made a difference.
We may wonder if our prayers mattered.
We may wonder if our kindness was received.
We may wonder if our obedience produced fruit.

But God's Word gives us this beautiful promise: **our labor is not in vain in the Lord.**

When something is done for Jesus, it has eternal value. People may forget, results may be slow, and fruit may be hidden for a season, but God is faithful.

Nothing done for the Lord is wasted.

Lesson: Faithful Service Has Eternal Value

First Corinthians 15:58 tells us to be steadfast, unmovable, and always abounding in the work of the Lord. This means we are called to keep standing, keep serving, and keep trusting God.

The word **steadfast** reminds us to stay faithful even when things are difficult.
The word **unmovable** reminds us not to be shaken from obedience.
The phrase **always abounding** reminds us to continue growing in the Lord's work.

This does not mean we never get tired or discouraged. It means we do not let discouragement have the final word. We keep our eyes on Jesus.

Some labor is seen quickly.
Some labor takes time.
Some labor is hidden.
Some labor may not be fully understood until eternity.

A prayer prayed in secret may strengthen someone more than you know.
A word of encouragement may keep someone from giving up.
A meal prepared in love may remind someone they are not forgotten.
A Bible lesson taught faithfully may plant seeds for generations.
A small act of kindness may become a testimony of God's love.

You may not always see the harvest immediately, but God sees every seed.

Key Truth

Nothing done for the Lord is wasted.

My labor has purpose when it is done in Him, through Him, and for His glory.

Bible Reading

Read the following Scriptures slowly and prayerfully:

1 Corinthians 15:58
Galatians 6:9
Hebrews 6:10
Psalm 126:5–6
Matthew 25:21

Reflection: God Sees Every Seed

Serving the Lord is often like planting seeds.

When a seed is planted, it disappears beneath the soil. For a while, it may look like nothing is happening. But hidden under the surface, life is beginning to grow.

In the same way, your service may not always show quick results. Your prayers may feel hidden. Your kindness may seem unnoticed. Your obedience may feel small.

But God is working beneath the surface.

Do not despise the season of hidden growth. Do not stop planting good seeds just because you cannot yet see the harvest.

The Lord knows how to bring fruit from faithful obedience.

Keep serving.
Keep praying.
Keep loving.
Keep giving.
Keep encouraging.
Keep obeying.

Your labor is not in vain.

Bible Study Questions

1. According to 1 Corinthians 15:58, what are believers called to be?

2. What does it mean to you that your labor is "not in vain in the Lord"?

3. Have you ever served faithfully but felt like you did not see results? Explain.

4. Read Galatians 6:9. What encouragement does this verse give when we feel weary?

5. Why is it important to keep serving even when the fruit is not visible yet?

6. Read Hebrews 6:10. What does this verse teach you about God's memory of your service?

____

____

____

7. What "seeds" have you been planting through prayer, kindness, service, or obedience?

____

____

____

8. What is one area where God is asking you to remain steadfast?

____

____

____

Heart Check

Take a moment and prayerfully ask yourself:

Do I become discouraged when I do not see quick results?
Do I believe God is working beneath the surface?
Am I willing to keep planting good seeds?
Have I allowed disappointment to slow down my obedience?

Do I trust God with the harvest?
Am I remaining steadfast in the work of the Lord?

Personal Application

This week, write down one area where you have been serving, praying, or obeying without seeing much fruit yet.

____

____

____

Now write a prayer of trust, giving the results to God:

____

____

____

Weekly Challenge

This week, do one act of faithful service as a seed planted for the Lord.

You may:

Pray for someone again.
Encourage someone again.
Serve your family with love.
Help someone quietly.
Teach or share God's Word faithfully.

Give kindness without expecting anything back.
Complete an assignment God placed before you.

Afterward, write what God reminded you:

____

____

____

Prayer

Lord Jesus,

Thank You for the promise that my labor is not in vain in You.
Help me when I feel discouraged. Help me when I cannot see
the fruit. Help me when I wonder if my service matters.

Teach me to be steadfast and unmovable. Teach me to keep
planting seeds of love, prayer, kindness, obedience, and faith.

I trust You with the harvest. I trust You with the timing. I trust
You with the results.

Let everything I do for You bring glory to Your name.

In Jesus' name,
Amen.

Declaration of Faith

My labor is not in vain in the Lord.
God sees every seed I plant.
God remembers my work and love.
I will remain steadfast.
I will not give up because fruit is hidden.
I trust God with the harvest.
Nothing done for Jesus is wasted.
I will keep serving with a willing heart.

Notes

Week 12:
Lord, Use Me

Main Scripture

"Also I heard the voice of the Lord, saying, Whom shall I send, and who will go for us? Then said I, Here am I; send me."
— Isaiah 6:8 KJV

Memory Verse

"Here am I; send me."
— Isaiah 6:8 KJV

Opening Prayer

Lord Jesus,

Thank You for calling me to serve You with a willing heart. Thank You for every lesson You have taught me through this Bible study.

Today, I surrender myself again to You. Use my life for Your glory. Use my hands to help, my words to encourage, my prayers to strengthen, and my heart to love others well.

Lord, wherever You lead me, help me say yes.

In Jesus' name,
Amen.

Opening Thought

A willing heart is one of the most beautiful offerings we can give to God.

After learning about serving, faithfulness, humility, hidden work, helping, weariness, and eternal rewards, the final question becomes personal:

"Lord, am I willing?"

Isaiah answered the call of God by saying, **"Here am I; send me."** He did not have every detail. He did not know everything that would happen. But he made himself available to the Lord.

God can do mighty things through a woman who is available, obedient, and willing.

Lesson: A Life Available to God

When Isaiah heard the voice of the Lord asking, **"Whom shall I send?"**, his answer was simple and surrendered:

"Here am I; send me."

This is the heart of a servant.

A servant does not always know the full assignment, but she trusts the One who is calling her. She may not feel perfect, fully ready, or completely strong, but she knows that God is faithful.

God is not looking for a heart full of pride.
He is looking for a heart willing to obey.
God is not looking for someone who wants glory for herself.
He is looking for someone who wants to glorify Him.

A willing servant says:

"Lord, use my life."
"Lord, use my story."
"Lord, use my gifts."
"Lord, use my pain for purpose."
"Lord, use my hands."
"Lord, use my words."
"Lord, use me wherever You place me."

Your service may not look like someone else's service, and that is okay. God knows exactly how He created you. He knows your gifts, your experiences, your testimony, your compassion, and your assignment.

When you place your life in His hands, He can use every part for His glory.

Key Truth

A willing heart gives God room to work through an obedient life.

The greatest service begins with a simple yes to the Lord.

Bible Reading

Read the following Scriptures slowly and prayerfully:

Isaiah 6:8
Romans 12:1
Matthew 9:37–38
2 Timothy 2:21
Psalm 25:4–5

Reflection: Saying Yes to God

Saying yes to God does not mean we will never feel afraid. It does not mean we will never have questions. It does not mean the assignment will always be easy.

Saying yes means we trust the Lord more than we trust our fears.

Sometimes yes looks like serving in church.
Sometimes yes looks like forgiving someone.
Sometimes yes looks like encouraging a hurting woman.
Sometimes yes looks like teaching God's Word.
Sometimes yes looks like helping quietly.
Sometimes yes looks like resting when God tells us to rest.
Sometimes yes looks like stepping out in faith.

God may use you in big ways, small ways, visible ways, or hidden ways. But every yes matters when it is given to Him.

A willing heart does not say, "Lord, use me only if people notice."
A willing heart says, "Lord, use me for Your glory."

Bible Study Questions

1. According to Isaiah 6:8, what did Isaiah say when the Lord asked, "Whom shall I send?"

2. What does the phrase "Here am I; send me" mean to you personally?

3. Why do you think availability is important in serving the Lord?

4. Read Romans 12:1. How does surrender connect with service?

5. What fear or hesitation sometimes keeps you from saying yes to God?

6. Read Matthew 9:37–38. What did Jesus say about
the harvest and the laborers?

7. What gift, testimony, or experience do you want
God to use for His glory?

8. What is one step of obedience God may be asking
you to take after this Bible study?

Heart Check

Take a moment and prayerfully ask yourself:

Am I available to the Lord?
Am I willing to serve even if the assignment is small?
Am I willing to serve even if the assignment is hidden?
Am I willing to obey even when I feel afraid?

Am I willing to let God use my gifts and my story?
Can I honestly say, "Lord, here am I; send me"?

Personal Application

Write your personal "yes" to the Lord.

Lord, I am willing to serve You by:

____

____

____

Lord, I surrender this area of my life to You:

____

____

____

Lord, use me to bless others in this way:

____

____

____

Weekly Challenge

This week, pray Isaiah 6:8 every morning:

"Lord, here am I; send me."

Then ask God to show you one person to encourage, help, pray for, or serve.

At the end of the week, write what happened:

____

____

____

Prayer

Lord Jesus,

Here I am. Use me.

Use my life for Your glory. Use my hands to serve, my words to encourage, my prayers to strengthen, my testimony to give hope, and my heart to love others.

I surrender my plans, my fears, my gifts, my time, and my service to You. Teach me to obey You with humility and faith.

Send me where You want me to go. Show me who You want me to help. Lead me in the way You want me to serve.

Let my life be a willing offering to You.

In Jesus' name,
Amen.

Declaration of Faith

Here I am, Lord. Use me.
My life belongs to Jesus.
My gifts belong to Jesus.
My service belongs to Jesus.
I will not hide from the call of God.
I will serve with humility and love.
I will say yes to the Lord.
My willing heart is an offering to Him.

Final Reflection for the 12-Week Journey

Over these 12 weeks, I have learned that serving the Lord is not about being seen, praised, or placed above others. It is about loving Jesus and obeying Him with a willing heart.

God sees small things.
God sees hidden things.
God sees faithful things.
God sees tired servants.
God sees labor done in love.
God sees the heart.

Write one truth from this Bible study that you want to carry with you:

____

____

____

Write one way you want to continue serving the Lord:

____

____

____

Closing Prayer for the Bible Study

Lord Jesus,

Thank You for walking with me through this study. Thank You for teaching me that every act of service matters when it is done for You.

Help me continue serving with joy, humility, faithfulness, and love. Keep my heart pure. Keep my hands willing. Keep my eyes fixed on You.

Let my life bring glory to Your name. Let my service bless others. Let my obedience be pleasing to You.

I give You my willing heart.

In Jesus' name,
Amen.

Notes

Final Encouragement

My dear sister in Christ,

As you come to the end of this 12-week Bible study, may your heart be reminded of this beautiful truth: **your service matters to God.**

Every prayer, every act of kindness, every quiet sacrifice, every helping hand, every word of encouragement, and every small assignment done for the Lord is precious in His sight.

You may not always be seen by people, but you are always seen by God.

He sees when you serve with tired hands.
He sees when you love through disappointment.
He sees when you keep praying.
He sees when you help quietly.
He sees when you choose humility.
He sees when you obey Him in hidden places.

Nothing done for Jesus is wasted.

Serving the Lord does not require a perfect life. It requires a willing heart. God can use your gifts, your testimony, your compassion, your hands, your words, and your everyday obedience for His glory.

Do not despise small assignments. Do not compare your calling to someone else's. Do not give up when the work feels unnoticed. The Lord who called you is faithful, and He will strengthen you as you continue to serve Him.

Keep serving with love.
Keep serving with humility.
Keep serving with joy.
Keep serving with faithfulness.
Keep serving with a willing heart.

May your life be a beautiful offering to Jesus.

May your service bless others.

May your obedience bring glory to God.

And may your heart always be ready to say:

"Lord, here am I. Use me."

"Therefore, my beloved brethren, be ye stedfast, unmoveable, always abounding in the work of the Lord, forasmuch as ye know that your labour is not in vain in the Lord."
— 1 Corinthians 15:58 KJV

Certificate of Completion

This certificate is proudly presented to

____

for faithfully completing

Serving the Lord with a Willing Heart

A 12-Week Bible Study on Faithful Service for the Lord

May you continue to serve the Lord Jesus Christ with humility, joy, faithfulness, and love.

May your life be a willing offering to Him, and may everything you do bring glory to His name.

"And whatsoever ye do, do it heartily, as to the Lord, and not unto men."
— Colossians 3:23 KJV

Completed on this day:

____

Presented by:

____

About the Author

Dr. Lende Click is a Christian author, counselor, Bible study teacher, speaker, and women's jail ministry servant who writes faith-filled books to encourage women, children, and families to grow closer to Jesus Christ.

Her writing is rooted in her love for the Lord and her desire to help others find healing, courage, hope, and purpose through God's Word. She is the author of several Christian books, Bible studies, devotionals, children's books, and inspirational works.

Dr. Click is an NCCA Licensed Professional Clinical Counselor, Certified Temperament Counselor, Licensed Clinical Pastoral Counselor, and Licensed Christian Counselor. She is also Advanced Certified in Death and Grief Therapy and Advanced Certified in Integrated Marriage and Family Therapy. Her counseling ministry focuses on helping individuals, women, marriages, families, and those walking through grief, trauma, stress, and life challenges.

She enjoys teaching women in Bible study and Sunday School, serving in women's ministry, ministering to women through jail ministry, and encouraging others to walk boldly in their God-given purpose.

Through her books and ministry, Dr. Click's heart is to remind every reader that God sees them, loves them, and can use their life for His glory.

Some proceeds from her books help support children in Cebu, Philippines.

Other Books by Dr. Lende Click

Thank you for reading **Serving the Lord with a Willing Heart**. If this Bible study encouraged you, you may also enjoy these other books by Dr. Lende Click:

Bible Studies, Devotionals, and Inspirational Books

Daughters of the King

Prayers of a Daughter of the King

God Is Still Writing Your Story

When God Carries a Woman Through the Fire

Healing for the Woman Who Has Been Hurt

The Gift of Godly Friendship

A Life Redeemed

Children's Books

Sammy the Shy Snail's Big Race

Bella the Brave Butterfly and the Stormy Day

Toby the Turtle Who Trusted God

Delen's Story: Faith Like Sunshine

Christian Fantasy

The Kingdom of Everlight

May every book encourage your heart, strengthen your faith, and remind you that God is still working in your life.